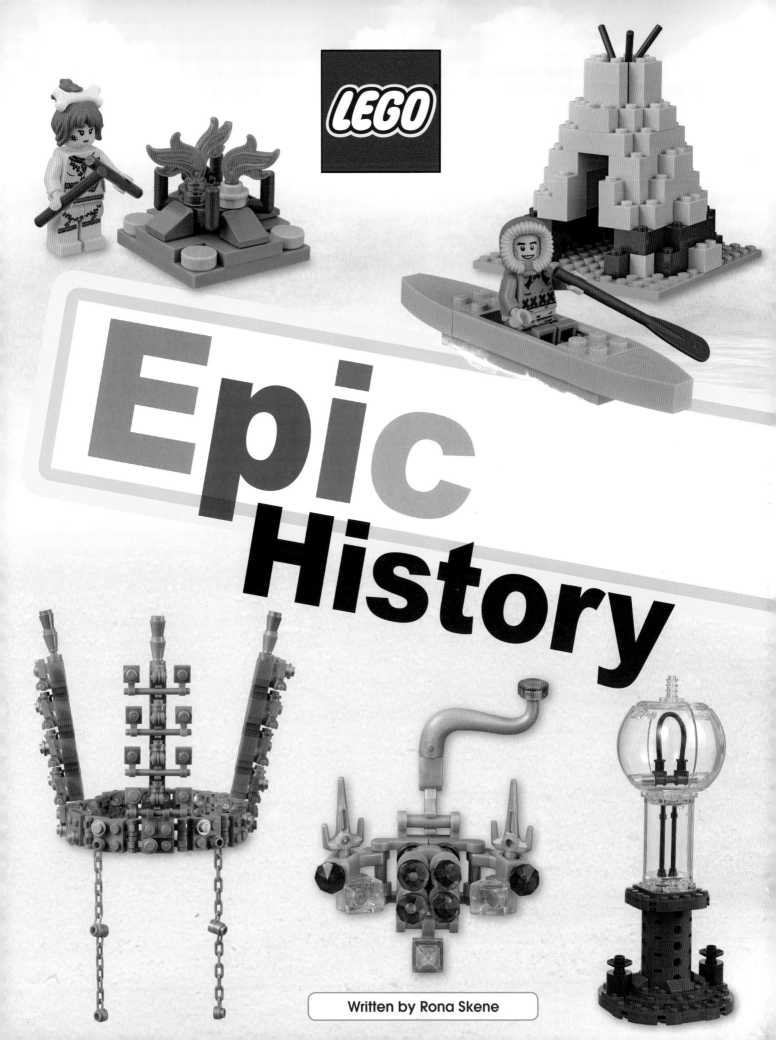

LEGO

Epic History

Written by Rona Skene

DK | Penguin Random House

Project Editor Beth Davies
Project Art Editor Jenny Edwards
US Editor Megan Douglass
Designer Stefan Georgiou
Editorial Assistant Nicole Reynolds
Pre-Production Producer Siu Yin Chan
Producer Lloyd Robertson
Managing Editor Paula Regan
Managing Art Editor Jo Connor
Publisher Julie Ferris
Art Director Lisa Lanzarini
Publishing Director Mark Searle

Inspirational models built by Jason Briscoe,
Nate Dias, and Simon Pickard
History consultant Philip Parker
Photography by Gary Ombler

Dorling Kindersley would like to thank Randi Sørensen,
Heidi K. Jensen, Paul Hansford, Martin Leighton
Lindhardt, Charlotte Neidhardt, Henk van der Does,
Nina Koopmann, and Torben Vad Nissen at the
LEGO Group. Also, at DK, Tori Kosara for additional
text; Lisa Stock and Ruth Amos for editorial assistance;
and Julia March for proofreading and index.

First American Edition, 2020
Published in the United States by DK Publishing
1450 Broadway, Suite 801, New York, NY 10018

Page design copyright ©2020 Dorling Kindersley Limited
DK, a Division of Penguin Random House LLC
20 21 22 23 24 10 9 8 7 6 5 4 3 2 1
001–316371–May/2020

A catalog record for this book
is available from the Library of Congress.
ISBN: 978-1-4654-9611-9

Printed and bound in China

**A WORLD OF IDEAS:
SEE ALL THERE IS TO KNOW**

www.LEGO.com
www.dk.com

Contents

The ancient world

HOME IS WHEREVER I BUILD MY FIRE.

From the earliest times, humans have been inventors. First, we discovered how to make fire and tools. Then, we used these tools to build villages that grew into cities, and ships that could explore the world around us. We also learned to write and use numbers.

Flames scared away wild animals ...

1 million years ago
Fire!
Our ancestors discovered how to make and use fire for keeping warm and cooking food.

3200 BCE
Wheely big news
Nobody is sure who first invented the wheel, but the earliest evidence of carts with wheels is from Mesopotamia.

Carts carried goods and people

3200 BCE
Word pictures
The Egyptians invented the world's first form of writing. Their system was a mixture of symbols and pictures, called hieroglyphs, that told a story.

Huge stones called megaliths

3000–1800 BCE
Stonehenge
This massive monument was built in Britain. Nobody knows exactly how and why it was built.

c.2600 BCE
Great pyramids
Pyramids were built as magnificent tombs for Egypt's rulers and their families.

c.2000 BCE
First calendar
Busy Mesopotamians invented a calendar that had 12 months of roughly 30 days each.

210 BCE
Terra-cotta Army
Qin Shih Huang Di, China's first emperor, was buried with an army of clay soldiers to protect him in the afterlife.

Soldier statues arranged in rows

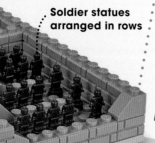

60 CE
Boudicca
In Britain, the queen of the Iceni people led a fight against the Roman invaders. Boudicca's name means "victorious"— but she lost, and the Romans stayed in Britain for 350 years!

117 CE
Mighty Romans
At its biggest, the Roman Empire ruled 60 million people, from Egypt to England.

Soldiers carried a flag called a standard

I'M ALWAYS ON THE MOVE! MY FEET HURT FROM MARCHING.

Build it!

A way to archway
Stacks of small LEGO® plates make up most of the gateway. A 1x1 curved tile is attached in the middle to create an arched walkway.

1x1 brick with side stud

1x1 curved tile

Thick fur coat

Large ivory tusks

300,000 BCE
Earliest humans
In Africa, the first modern humans roamed in family groups. They picked fruit and berries, and hunted large animals such as the woolly mammoth.

10,000 BCE
First farmers
Humans started to settle, keeping animals such as cows and goats and planting crops including wheat and barley.

Cattle kept for meat and milk

8000–5000 BCE
First metal tools
Early humans began to use copper to make tools. These tools were much sharper and more useful than stone ones.

C. 4000 BCE
Silkworms
In China, people made silk thread from the cocoons of silkworms.

Babylon's grand Ishtar Gate

4000 BCE
The first cities
In Mesopotamia, in today's Middle East, cities like Ur, and later Babylon, grew as farmers met and traded their goods.

C. 1500 BCE
Egyptian water clocks
The Egyptians marked time by measuring the water that dripped from a jar.

Stone jar with hole in the bottom

C. 1200 BCE
Iron Age
With the invention of iron, tools got even tougher and so did wheels. It meant farming was easier and vehicles could go further than before.

C. 1000 BCE
Phoenician sailors
Living by the Mediterranean Sea, Phoenician people were brilliant at shipbuilding. They traded with other countries and may even have sailed around Africa.

438 BCE
The Parthenon
The Greeks finished building a huge temple to honor the goddess Athena, the protector of the city of Athens.

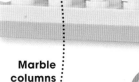

Marble columns

4x4 round plate

Build it!

Looks round
Give a suggestion of a bowl's round shape by placing angled plates on four sides of a round blue plate.

1x2 brick with side studs

2x2 double angled plate

Early humans

The first humans lived in Africa. They found food by hunting, fishing, and picking wild plants. Over time, they learned how to build shelters, create fire, and make tools. Early humans also developed the world's first language, so they could tell each other about their lives!

Ax heads tied to wooden handles with animal skin

Sharp spears for hunting animals

▲ Making tools

People turned flint rocks into tools. They used rounded stones to flake bits off the rocks and give them sharp edges. These tools could then be used for building and hunting.

Key moments

120,000 BCE Some humans left Africa and found new places to live. Those who moved to cooler places **made clothes** out of animal skins.

40,000 BCE People began painting. They used **twigs and feathers** to paint pictures of the animals they hunted.

YUM! BBQ MAMMOTH FOR DINNER!

Sticks rubbed together to make sparks

Fire light ▶

Humans discovered how to make and use fire around 1 million years ago. Now they had heat to keep them warm and cook food, and light to help them hunt and find shelter at night.

Fire lined with rocks

Hole in one!
The mammoth tusks slot into elements with holes. Use as many tusks as you want to form a curved shelter.

Bone attaches to plates with clips

Build it!

.... Round tile with hole

Mammoth tusks make curved roof

▶ Finding shelter
When out hunting, people built shelters out of rocks, bones, wood, and animal skins to keep them warm and dry. The shelters were quick and easy to take down and rebuild at the next camp.

OOPS, DIDN'T MEAN TO DISTURB YOU ... NICE KITTY ...

▶ Saber-tooth cat
This beast was also called the Smilodon, but don't mistake its big teeth for a smile! Saber-tooth cats would attack much larger animals by leaping out of trees and landing on them.

Curved fangs, 12 in (30 cm) long

.... Huge paws with sharp claws

People picked wild fruits, berries, and herbs ....

Clip it together
Build it!

Plates with clips are the foundation of the basket's sides. Layer plates and grilles over the plates with clips to create a basketlike texture.

Attach plates with clips vertically

1x2 grilles connect to 1x4 plate

◀ Finding food
People made baskets by weaving plants or twigs together. Baskets made it easier and quicker to gather food. They were so tightly woven that water could be stored in them.

Baskets made from nettles, bark, and grasses

2x2 plate with bars

Pyramids of Giza ▼

The largest pyramid ever built is the Great Pyramid of Giza. It was built as a tomb for the pharaoh Khufu who ruled Egypt 5,000 years ago. The Great Pyramid is still standing today, surrounded by a group of similar, but slightly smaller, structures.

Ancient Egypt

The lush banks of the mighty Nile River were once home to an ancient civilization that lasted thousands of years. The Ancient Egyptians left behind some truly awesome monuments, as well as fascinating objects and writing.

Build it!

1x2 slope peak

1x4 slope

Pyramid scheme

Varying sizes of slope bricks form the iconic pyramid shape. Use smaller slope bricks at the top.

Inside the pyramid are tunnels, a grand gallery, and burial chambers

▼ Sailing the Nile

On the Nile River, people fished in boats called skiffs. These light boats were made from woven stems of papyrus, a tall grass that grew along the banks of the river.

THERE'S A SNAKE IN MY BOAT!

Fish trapped in a net made from willow branches

The Sphinx is longer than six buses and taller than a house

THE SPHINX WAS ALREADY 2,500 YEARS OLD WHEN I WAS BORN!

Cleopatra was pharaoh from 51 BCE to 30 BCE

Key moments

c. 1500 BCE Work began on the Valley of the Kings, a **network of underground tombs**. More than 60 royal tombs, many still full of treasures, have since been found at this site.

1473 BCE Hatshepsut was one of the **few female pharaohs**. She reigned for 21 years and made Egypt rich by trading with nearby countries instead of fighting with them.

▲ The Great Sphinx

A sphinx is a mythical creature with the body of a lion and the head of a human. The Great Sphinx of Giza was built out of limestone 4,500 years ago, to guard the tomb of the pharaoh Khafre.

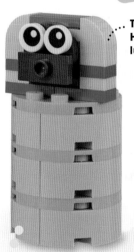

The jackal god Duamutef guards the stomach

The baboon god Hapi guards the lungs

◄ Canopic jars

When a person's body was made into a mummy, some of the organs were taken out and stored separately in special containers called canopic jars. Each jar had a different lid, to show which god was guarding it.

Bandages made of linen

◄ Cat mummy

When an important person or animal died, the body was "mummified." The bodies were dried with salt, treated with chemicals, then carefully wrapped in bandages.

Cats were worshipped by Egyptians, who also kept them as pets

1x2 brick with side studs

Eyes and mouth connect to a round 2x2 plate

1x1 bricks with arches form the sides and back of this headdress

Build it!

About face

Bricks with side studs enable sideways connections. Build bricks with side studs into the headdresses of your jars so you can create faces.

Tiered seats gave everyone a good view

Ancient Greece

At its peak, Ancient Greece was the richest, most powerful state there had ever been in Europe—and the cleverest, too. Ancient Greeks are famous for philosophy, science, history books, the theater, and the Olympic Games!

MAKE WAY— COMING THROUGH!

Key moments

461 BCE Pericles became **leader of the city of Athens**. He led the navy, introduced new laws, and had grand buildings and temples built.

387 BCE The Academy, one of the **first universities**, was founded. Students studied philosophy and astronomy as well as working out in the gymnasium.

Brightly colored clay decorated with black paint

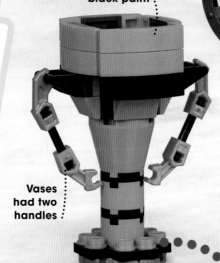

Vases had two handles

Pottery making ▲
The Greeks made pottery out of clay. These vessels could be used to store wine, olive oil, and honey. Vases and other containers were often painted with scenes from action-packed stories.

▲ Racing chariots
Chariot racing was a very popular sport. Huge crowds watched up to 40 chariots race around a track called a hippodrome. Collisions and crashes were common!

Build it!

Upside-down 3x3 cone brick

Going up
Use conical pieces to replicate the shape of the pot, which goes from wide at the top to narrow at the bottom.

Olympia's stadium had stone seats for 45,000 people

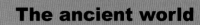

Build it!

2x2 double axle plate

Cart wheel

Two-wheel drive
Both of the chariot's wheels connect to a 2x2 axle plate. This sits under the chariot's body for a smooth, level ride.

▲ Watching sports
Greek people gathered to watch sports in huge stadiums. The first stadium was built at Olympia for the ancient Olympic Games. Contestants competed on a clay track.

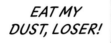

EAT MY DUST, LOSER!

Driver stood behind a protective shield

Chariots made of wood and leather

... Racing chariots had two or four horses

Wooden wheels with tough strips of metal as tires

Myths and legends

Trojan horse
Legend says that the Ancient Greeks pulled a trick on their old rivals the Trojans, who lived in the city of Troy. Clever Greek warrior Odysseus gave the Trojans a present of a huge wooden horse. The horse was actually full of soldiers, who crept out in the night, opened the city gates, and let the rest of the Greek army in!

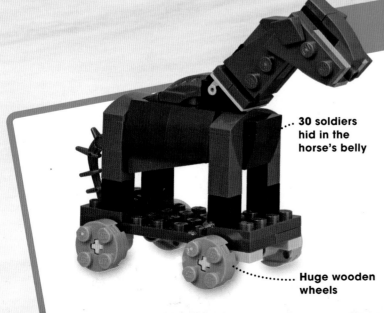

30 soldiers hid in the horse's belly

Huge wooden wheels

> AFTER A LONG DAY OF HARVESTING RICE, I AM HUNGRY FOR A BOWL OF MORE RICE!

Ancient China

For centuries, the part of Asia that would become China was made up of kingdoms that were constantly battling each other. Then, in 221 BCE, general Ying Zheng seized control of the whole region. The new ruler called himself Qin Shih Huang Di, which means "First Emperor."

▼ In the fields

Rice was the most commonly eaten food in southern China. Rice was grown in flooded ground called paddy fields. In hilly areas, these fields were laid out in layers and called rice terraces. Rice is still grown in paddy fields today.

Rice planted in neat rows to make harvesting easier

Build it!

1x2 plate

1x1 plate with ring

Bar

Cart wheel

Let's roll!

A bar slides through the wheel and two 1x1 plates with rings. You can attach it by connecting the plates with rings to 1x2 plates on the wheelbarrow's underside.

You couldn't harvest rice without getting your feet wet!

◄ Wheelbarrow

Wheelbarrows were invented in Ancient China to help farmers transport goods. They were known at the time as "wooden oxen."

Long handles make pulling the wheelbarrow easier

Large central wheel carries the weight

Sentries guarded the wall from watchtowers

The wall was wide enough for soldiers to march along the top

▶ Great Wall

The new emperor built a huge wall along China's northern border to keep out invaders. Later emperors added to the wall until, by the 1500s, it was 5,550 miles (8,850 km) long!

Umbrella provides shelter from the rain and sun

▲ Transportation

Rich people and government officials traveled in chariots pulled by one or two horses. The carriages had large wheels, which gave the passengers a smooth ride.

Key moment

132 CE Inventor Zhang Heng designed one of the first-ever seismoscopes—an **earthquake detector** that gave early warning of quakes. It could detect tremors up to 400 miles (640 km) away.

Myths and legends

Special creatures

To the Ancient Chinese, dragons weren't scary—they were symbols of power, wisdom, and good luck. People believed that their emperors were descended from dragons, and that mountain ranges were the backs of giant dragons, asleep underground.

A dragon with the teeth of a lion and the claws of an eagle

Ancient Rome

Key moments

27 BCE Army general Octavian became Augustus, **the first Emperor of Rome**.

80 CE The Colosseum in Rome was completed. It was the **biggest sporting arena** ever seen. The first games that took place there lasted 100 days!

Rome grew from a few small settlements on the banks of the Tiber River into a great city ... and then kept on growing! The mighty Roman army marched across Europe and beyond. By 117 CE, Rome's empire stretched over two million square miles (five million square kilometers).

Soldiers often marched 18 miles (30 km) in a day

Marble columns with beautiful decorations

Different rooms for hot, warm, or cold baths

WE'LL BE IN LONDINIUM BY LUNCHTIME!

▲ Public baths

Every Roman town had a grand bath house, where people went to meet, relax, and exercise, as well as to get clean. The baths were heated by hot air from huge furnaces under the floor.

Roadside ditches to funnel rainwater

◄ Super highway

The Romans built long, straight, smooth roads to help the army get around the empire. The roads were built with crushed rock topped with stone, and they sloped so that water ran off the surface.

▶ Awesome aqueduct

Rome's expert engineers built huge, arched bridges called aqueducts to bring fresh water to their cities from lakes and rivers far away.

Aqueducts cross valleys to transport water to higher ground

Water runs in a stone channel along the top of the bridge

People ate lying down on large couches

1x1 brick with side stud

Floor to ceiling
Attach the 1x2 textured bricks of the wall to the floor using 1x1 bricks with side studs.

Build it!

▲ Grand banquet

Rich Romans loved to feast! A grand banquet might have started in the afternoon and carried on until midnight! Roman treats included camel heels, peacock brains, nightingales, and dormice.

Dishes were laid out on low tables

Myths and legends

The wolf fed the babies as if they were her own cubs

Romulus and Remus
According to myth, the city of Rome was founded by twin brothers Romulus and Remus. As babies, they were left by a river and found by a wolf. The wolf took them to her cave and cared for them until they were taken in by a kind shepherd.

The Middle Ages

The Middle Ages were a time of turmoil, with mighty rulers competing to expand their empires and grow richer. This period was also a time of learning, with many important inventions and discoveries made, as well as beautiful art that we can still see today.

Camels carried gold across the Sahara Desert

600–700
Gold in Ghana
In West Africa, the Kingdom of Ghana grew rich by building huge iron and gold mines. Ghana traded the precious metals with other countries in Africa and Europe.

1021
Early tale
The earliest known novel was written by Murasaki Shikibu, a Japanese lady-in-waiting.

1066
Normans conquer England
Duke William of Normandy and his French army landed in Britain and defeated King Harold to claim the English throne.

1025
Medical marvel
Avicenna, a Persian doctor, published a medical textbook that would be used by doctors for hundreds of years.

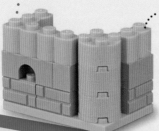

The Normans built stone castles all over England

Magnetic needle always points north

c.1100
Magnetic compass
Chinese scientists invented a compass that used the Earth's magnetism to help travelers find their way.

1206–1294
Mongols rule
Led by Genghis Khan, the Mongols of East Asia built the world's largest empire.

1347–1352
Black Death
The Black Death was one of the deadliest diseases ever. In six years it had wiped out more than half of the people in Europe.

Fleas on rats carried the disease

1368
China's Great Wall
The emperor extended China's ancient defensive wall to make it the longest human-made structure in the world. It was around 5,550 miles (8,850 km) long!

1420
Seeing stars
In Samarkand, Uzbekistan, the Mongol king Ulugh Beg built the world's largest observatory. It made many new studies of the stars and planets.

c.1420
European culture
Artists and scholars in Italy began copying ideas from Ancient Greece and Rome. This movement spread through all of Europe and was called the Renaissance.

Painting, sculpture, and buildings were all part of the Renaissance

Step right up!
Create temple steps by attaching plates with bars to plates with clips. Connect your staircases to a brick with studs.

1x1 plate with clip

1x1 brick with studs

1x2 plate with bar

Build it!

Viking warrior woman c.900

The Maya built huge stone temples—some are still standing!

600–900
Mayan cities
The Maya of Central America were the first people in America to invent a way of writing using symbols. They were also expert astronomers.

793
Viking invasion
Viking sailors from Scandinavia landed their first longships in Britain. They ruled parts of the country for the next 300 years.

Round wooden shield

The settlers built huge stone heads called moai

800–1200
Easter Island
Explorers from the Pacific Polynesian Islands settled on Easter Island, off the coast of South America.

1000
First fireworks
The first firecrackers were made in China. Hollow bamboo stems were packed with gunpowder and thrown onto bonfires.

Rockets had tissue-paper fuses

1271
Marco Polo
Italian explorer Marco Polo set off on his journey to China. He later introduced Chinese inventions to Europe for the first time.

1289
First glasses
In Italy, a monk wrote about the first eyeglasses. They were made from two magnifying lenses joined together, which were held over the nose.

Lenses made from thick quartz

1325
Mali Empire
The ancient city of Timbuktu was made part of the Mali Empire. The empire's ruler, Mansa Musa, is thought to be the richest person who ever lived.

1325–1521
Aztec Empire
The mighty Aztecs were not only fierce warriors but skilled farmers and craftspeople. Mexico City is built on top of the ruins of the great Aztec city of Tenochtitlan.

The Aztecs invented drinking chocolate

Mali had rich reserves of gold

Frame it
Build an A-frame for your easel by connecting two 1x8 plates with a 1x4 panel and a 2x2 hinge plate.

2x2 hinge plate

1x4 panel

Build it!

Move a head
Give the dragon some bite! Plates with clips attach to a plate with bar to allow hingelike jaw movement.

1x2 plate with bar

1x1 plate with clip

Build it!

Woolen sails coated in grease to make them waterproof

◄ Battle ship
Wooden longships were built to be strong enough to sail on the stormiest seas, but light enough to carry when the Viking raiding party hit dry land. They had sails as well as oars, and could carry about 80 people.

Carved dragon's head

A longship could have up to 34 oars

Longhouse ►
Vikings built their houses long, just like their ships. Several families lived in one large, narrow house. In winter, it got even more crowded when their cattle moved in, too!

Roof covered with straw or turf

Where in the world?

The Vikings

Iron strip to protect the nose

Raider's helmet ▲
Viking helmets didn't have horns—that would have made them too easy to knock off! They were made of iron plates lined with leather and wool to make them more comfortable.

The Vikings from Norway, Sweden, and Denmark were skillful sailors, expert shipbuilders, and fierce warriors! They used their skills to sail long distances discovering and conquering new lands.

The nobleman and his family lived in the top story

Medieval Japan

▲ Great castle

Rich noblemen built grand, towering castles to defend their lands. The largest was called Himeji Castle, and it is still standing today.

Wealthy clans in Medieval Japan were constantly battling over land and power. The most powerful general, the Shogun, ruled with the help of his Samurai army. This period in Japan's history is also famous for its stunning art and buildings.

Key moment

1192 General Minamoto Yoritomo became **Japan's first Shogun**. The emperor was still officially in charge, but for a time the Shogun made the important decisions.

Top crossbeam is called a kasagi

Torii made from stone or wood

Armor made of metal, wood, and leather

◀ Samurai armor

Samurai were loyal, fearless soldiers. Their amazing armor was made from hundreds of small pieces linked together. They wore masks to hide their face and scare their enemies.

▲ Shinto gateway

Shinto is the most ancient religion of Japan. Its followers believe in nature spirits called kami. Shinto shrines are entered through beautiful gateways called torii.

Kusazuri flaps to protect the legs

Early North America

For much of North American history, the continent was home to groups of native people. Just as the land was vast and varied, these groups all had their own ways of life. People lived in different types of homes and searched for different types of food, depending on the climate.

Key moments

c. 25,000 BCE The very first Americans originally came from Asia. They crossed a **narrow strip of land** (which is now under the sea) into Alaska, then moved down through the continent.

c. 950 CE In Mississippi, people begin building a **gigantic earth pyramid** now called Monks Mound. It's wider than Egypt's Great Pyramid, and you can still see it today.

Inuit igloo ▼

A group called the Inuit lived in the cold north of North America, as their descendants still do today. The Inuit hunted for whales, seals, and huge deer called caribou. When they were on a hunt they made shelters, called igloos, out of snow.

Walls made from blocks of tightly-packed snow

Narrow entrance kept out the cold

I WISH I'D PACKED MY GLOVES!

▼ Hunter's kayak

The Inuit invented a light, sealskin canoe called a kayak. These were designed to be fast, so the hunter could paddle at top speed in pursuit of seals or walruses.

Whalebone or wood frame

1x2 brick with side studs

Smooth sailing
Tiles, which attach to 1x2 bricks with side studs, give the kayak smooth sides.

1x3 curved slope

1x6 tile

Build it!

◄ Cozy camp

Some groups of native people lived in tents called tepees. The tents were cool in summer and warm in winter, and were easy to move when people set up new camps and villages.

Frame made with wooden poles tied at the top ……

Animal skins sewn together to make the cover

Totem poles show real and mythical animals and family ancestors

The thunderbird is believed to flap its wings to create thunder ……

Build it!

Stack 'em up

A 1x1 plate is positioned in the center of the top of each head. This enables you to stack another head on top.

1x1 plate ……

Totem pole ►

People in the northwest carved tree trunks into tall totem poles for their villages. The beautiful carvings told stories, celebrated special events, or honored past leaders.

Some group leaders wore feathered headdresses—symbols of great respect and honor

Corn kernels were dried and ground up into flour

WHAT A BUMPER CROP THIS IS!

Seedlings in neat rows

▲ Crop farming

Early Americans in the southwest were expert farmers. They dug canals to bring water to dry desert soil so they could grow beans, squash, and corn, which they nicknamed "the three sisters."

Baskets for gathering crops

The Silk Road

The Silk Road was actually lots of different routes that linked up to make a 4,350-mile- (7,000-km-) long route that stretched from Asia to Europe. The path got its name because merchants used it to transport luxurious goods, such as silk, between countries far away from each other.

Double row of eyelashes to keep sand out

Asian camels have two humps

Strong backs carry heavy loads

◀ Camel train

Tough, sure-footed camels were the best way to carry goods through the mountains and deserts of Asia. They traveled together in long lines called caravans.

Flat, wide feet don't sink into the sand

Build it!

A load off
Each camel's pack is built onto its body. The whole side panel attaches to bricks with side studs in the camel's belly!

Bricks with side studs

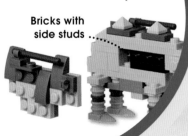

Sticks of cinnamon from Sri Lanka

Popular spices such as ginger, nutmeg, and pepper

Trading posts ▶

All along the Silk Road merchants met up to buy and sell their goods. Most traders didn't travel the whole route. They sold their cargo to someone else who would take it on to the next trading post.

LEGO® claw

Angles, ahoy!
The dhow's sails are made from white angled plates. They are held at an angle using a claw piece in a 1x1 plate with top clip.

Build it!

Square sails on multiple masts

Triangular sails

▲ Junk boat
Rather than traveling over land, some traders chose a faster but riskier way of transporting their goods across the China Sea. They sailed on large Chinese boats called junks.

Hull planks stitched together with rope

▲ Dhow boat
Arab traders used traditional narrow boats called dhows to carry cargo over the Indian Ocean to the Persian Gulf.

Beautiful Chinese pottery

For a long time only the Chinese knew how to make silk, so it was expensive to buy

Key moments

c.500-600 Spies managed to **smuggle silkworms** out of China, meaning that silk could finally be made elsewhere. It became a much less valuable trading item.

1279 When **Mongol leader Kublai Khan** took control of China, he sent his army along the Silk Road to make sure that merchants could travel the route safely.

Italian glass

Western merchants used silver and gold to trade for eastern goods

African empires

The enormous continent of Africa has contained many different kingdoms and empires over its long history. Some grew rich by carrying goods such as gold, ivory, ebony, and salt across the vast Sahara desert to trade with European and Arab merchants.

Stelae were up to 108 ft (33 m) tall

Carved granite looks like windows and a door

▲ Royal memorial

The Aksum kingdom grew rich by trading ivory, and was the most powerful East African state for many centuries. The Aksum built magnificent tall, carved structures called stelae to mark the tombs of their rulers.

Baked mud is also called adobe

Wooden beams strengthen the structure

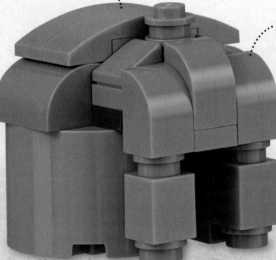

▲ Building blocks

Many buildings were built from mud baked in the sun to make solid bricks. The largest mudbrick building in the world was built in 1240 in Djenné, on the banks of the Niger River.

Making music ▶

Griots were musicians and entertainers in West Africa. They also told stories, making their drums "talk" by raising and lowering the sounds they made.

Squeezing strings on the side changes the sound

Build it!

Tied up with string

Four lightsaber hilt pieces hold this model together. The cone bricks that form the drum's body don't connect to each other.

Lightsaber hilt piece

2x2 round plate with hooks

Curved drumstick

Royal palace ▶

The enormous Gyeongbokgung Palace was first built in 1395 as the home of King Taejo and his family. In the 16th century, it burned down and was rebuilt. 300 years later it was destroyed by invaders and rebuilt again.

7,700 rooms in palace

Two-tiered curving roof

Tower made of 365 stones, one for each day of the year

29 ft (9 m) high

◀ Seeing stars

This stone tower is called Cheomseongdae and was used as an observatory. It was built in 640 and was used by ancient Korean astronomers to look at the night sky. It's still standing, making it the oldest surviving observatory in the world.

Key moment

668 King Munmu ended hundreds of years of conflict by **unifying the neighboring kingdoms** of Silla, Baekje, and Goguryeo under his rule.

▼ Signs of power

Silla rulers wore elaborate gold crowns, richly decorated with jewels. When kings and queens died, they were buried wearing their crowns, in tombs under huge mounds of rocks.

Gold prongs in treelike shapes

Where in the world?

Ancient Korea

When the ruler of a small kingdom called Silla defeated his neighboring cities and kingdoms, he joined them all to create the new country of Korea. Korea soon became rich by trading gold, silver, and furs with its neighbor, China.

Gold chains hang down from crown

Medieval Europe

During the Middle Ages in Europe, rulers and noblemen lived in splendid castles, sending their soldiers and knights to battle with their rivals. Ordinary people mostly lived on the noblemen's estates, working hard to grow food for themselves and their masters.

Peasant farmers ▼

People called peasants worked on farms owned by their masters. In exchange for their work, peasants each had a small patch of land to grow their own food and keep animals. Peasants were often not allowed to move away from where they were born.

Thatched roof

Walls made of a mixture of wood, straw, and clay, called wattle and daub

Fences to keep animals in pens and away from crops

THE LORD'S LATEST DEMAND IS THE LAST STRAW!

Two shafts to pull or push cart by

Large wheels to give a smooth ride over bumpy ground

▲ Getting around

Peasants used two-wheeled carts to transport straw and hay to and from the fields, or to carry tools. The carts could be pushed or pulled by a person, or hitched up to a horse for heavier loads.

1x4x2 fence with spindles ....

1x2 hinge brick ....

Build it!

Side angle

Give your cart angled sides by connecting fence pieces to 1x2 hinge bricks.

Thick stone walls with gaps for firing arrows

Guards kept lookout from tall towers

◄ Castle life

Noblemen built castles to live in and protect themselves from enemies. A castle was like a small village. As well as the lord and his family, it was home to servants, soldiers, craftsmen—and farm animals, too!

Narrow bridge to control entrance to the castle

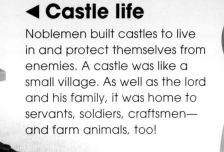

Build it!

Side shield

1x1 bricks with side studs fit into the horse's body to keep its shining armor in place.

1x1 brick with side stud

Long, blunt lance

Heavy suit of armor

> WAIT FOR ME, A HORSE NEEDS A RIDER!

▲ Jousting tournament

The joust was a contest of riding and fighting skills. Huge crowds watched as knights, representing their rich masters, rode toward each other. Each knight tried to knock the other off their horse with a wooden lance.

Carved wooden details

Grand throne ►

The ruler of a country or region sat on a magnificent throne—a symbol of their power and wealth. The throne room was often at the center of the palace or castle and raised on a platform.

Key moments

1215 In England, King John was forced to sign the Magna Carta. This document stated that there were **some limits on the king's powers** and that he could not be in charge of everything by himself.

1337 France and England began a war that lasted for **more than 100 years!**

Age of discovery

The world became linked in new ways as European adventurers set sail on their fast new ships for faraway lands full of natural wonders. And it wasn't just explorers who were busy; it was a time of exciting changes for scientists, inventors, architects, and artists, too.

375 ft (114.5 m) high dome

1471
Florence cathedral
The Italian cathedral's massive dome was finally complete. It had eight sides and was built from 4 million bricks.

1543
Studying the sun
Polish scientist Copernicus figured out that the Earth is not the center of the universe—our planet moves around the sun, not the other way around!

1543
King Henry VIII
English king Henry married his sixth wife, Catherine Parr, making him the most married English monarch ever.

1577
Stargazing
Taqi al-Din developed advanced instruments to view spectacular astronomical events, including the Great Comet of 1577. He later opened a huge observatory.

Chocolate was a luxury item

1585
Sweet treats
Spanish explorers brought cacao beans back from Central America. Europe got its first taste of chocolate!

1607
New to America
English settlers built their first permanent base in what is now the US. They called it Jamestown after the English King, James I.

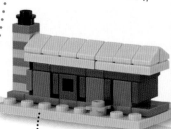

Homes were built inside a triangular fort

1666
Great Fire of London
In England's capital, a devastating fire started in a bakery in Pudding Lane. It destroyed 75% of the city, and 80,000 Londoners lost their homes.

Every pirate captain had their own flag design

1690
Jolly Roger
The skull-and-crossbones flag was first raised by French pirates. Soon, more pirates began to use it as a scary warning they were about to attack!

1723
Carnival in Brazil
Rio de Janeiro's first carnival was a very rowdy affair. Today, half a million people come to enjoy the world's biggest dance party.

THIS TIME PERIOD WILL INSPIRE SOME GREAT PLAYS!

English playwright William Shakespeare was born in 1564

1488
Around Africa
Bartolomeu Dias of Portugal was the first European to sail around a point in southern Africa, now called the Cape of Good Hope.

Leonardo called his design the aerial screw

1492
Hello America!
Italian explorer Christopher Columbus reached North America on a mission for Spain's king and queen.

1493
Leonardo's inventions
Renowned artist Leonardo da Vinci designed the first helicopter, although he never got around to building it!

1512–1520
Ottoman Empire
During the rule of fierce sultan Selim the Grim, the Turkish Ottomans conquered many lands, including Syria and Egypt.

Build it!

Sloped ship
Inverted slopes make the ship's curved hull, while white 1x1 slopes and 1x2 plates with slopes make the sails.

1x1 slope

1x2 plate with slope

1x2 inverted slope

Magellan's ship was called *Victoria*

1519–1522
Around the world
Ferdinand Magellan of Portugal led the first expedition to circle the world—and all because he wanted to find spices to sell at home!

Room for 20,000 people

1609–1616
Blue Mosque
This huge mosque got its nickname from its 20,000 blue tiles that shimmered in the Constantinople sunshine.

1610
Into the bay
Henry Hudson—an English explorer trying to find a route to China from Europe—entered Hudson Bay, now part of Canada.

1610–1611
Shakespeare's last play
England's most famous playwright wrote his final play, *The Tempest*—an enchanting tale of magic and shipwrecked sailors.

1635
Peacock Throne
Mughal emperor Shah Jahan (which means "King of the World") installed the fabulous, jewel-encrusted Peacock Throne at his palace, the Red Fort.

1635
Closed country
Japan begins a period when foreigners were banned from visiting for more than 200 years. It was a time of elegant cities, art, theater, and Sumo wrestling.

Build it!

Simple, but stately
Add ornate detail using gold pieces, transparent red panels, and two blue plates with shafts as a pair of birds on top!

1x1 plate with shaft

1x1 brick with scroll

Telescope piece

The throne contained the huge Koh-i-Noor diamond

Distinctive pagoda building style

WELCOME TO THE AZTEC WORLD!

Aztec civilization

The Aztecs were a fierce warrior tribe who ruled large parts of Mexico for more than 200 years. Their capital was the splendid island city of Tenochtitlan.

Pyramid was the tallest building in the city

Shrines to both gods at the top

Aztec temple ▶

The pyramid-shaped Great Temple was built to honor two Aztec gods—Huitzilopochtli, god of the sun and war, and Tlaloc, god of rain and farming.

Key moment

1325 The Aztecs founded Tenochtitlan, their **sacred city**. According to legend, it was built on the spot where the emperor saw an eagle struggling with a snake in its beak.

◀ Headdress

Top Aztec warriors wore huge headdresses to show their importance. They were decorated with jewels, gold, shells, and feathers.

250 bird feathers in emperor's headdress

52-ft- (16-m-) high walls

Stones expertly cut to fit together without gaps

◀ Llama helpers

The Inca didn't have wheeled vehicles—they used llamas instead! Llamas are sturdy and stable on their feet—perfect for lugging things up and down rocky mountains.

Thick, woolly fleece keeps out the cold

Padded feet grip on rocky paths

▲ Fortress walls

The stone walls of the fortress protecting the Inca city of Cusco are still standing today—showing how brilliant Inca builders were! The walls are built with bricks of different shapes and sizes that slot together perfectly, without the use of mortar to hold them in place.

Where in the world?

Key moment

1450 Emperor Pachacuti built the stone city of Machu Picchu, perched on a 8,200-ft- (2,500-m-) high mountaintop. It was largely **abandoned for 400 years**, but is now one of the world's most-visited places.

Inca Empire

The Inca people lived in the mountains of western South America. They were expert farmers, and also excellent engineers who built magnificent cities and thousands of miles of roads.

Mughal Empire

The Mughals ruled India for more than 300 years, after the first Mughal emperor, Babur, conquered large areas of land. Some of the world's most beautiful buildings were created by the Mughal people, who were also skilled at astronomy, science, and metalwork.

Cypress trees on either side of the lake

Key moments

1556 Akbar, one of the most powerful and successful Mughal emperors, came to the throne **aged just 13!**

1601 Akbar built the **Buland Darwaza** gate to celebrate one of his many victories in battle. At 177 ft (54 m) high, it is the tallest gate in the world.

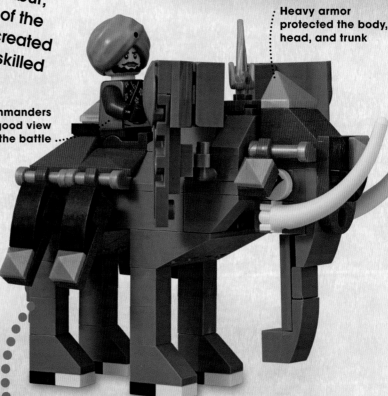

Army commanders had a good view of the battle

Heavy armor protected the body, head, and trunk

Elephant army ▲
Mughal armies had an awesome advantage over their enemies—elephants! When these armored giants charged at the enemy, alarmed troops would run for their lives!

Build it!

1x2/2x2 angle plate

Plate armor
You can connect the elephant's armor to its head and face by attaching an angle plate.

▼ Taj Mahal

Emperor Shah Jahan built this magnificent building in memory of his wife. It took 20,000 human workers—and 1,000 elephants to carry the marble and stone—more than 21 years to finish the project.

Walls are made of white marble

Towers are called minarets

Build it!

1x1 plate with bar

1x2 plate with clip ......

1x1 round brick

Master this
A simple stack of 1x1 round bricks and 1x1 plates with bars form the mast. Attach sails by using plates with clips.

A brooch called a sarpech was worn on a turban

◄ Fabulous jewels

Wealthy Mughals used diamonds, emeralds, sapphires, and other kinds of precious gems to make beautiful jewelry. They also used gems to decorate everything from dishes and goblets to swords and weapons.

Elsewhere in the world

Portuguese explorers

Sailors from Portugal were the first Europeans to meet the Mughals, arriving in small, speedy ships called caravels. These ships could sail long distances, making them the perfect craft for explorers and traders looking for new treasures to buy and sell.

Sails designed for changeable winds ...

Sturdy wooden hull to withstand storms ...

Time of learning

After the Middle Ages, new ideas started to spread, especially in the world of science. People began to base their ideas on what they could find out and test for themselves. This meant that inventors got busy, too, making new instruments to help scientists observe and measure the world around them.

Key moments

1570 Belgian mapmaker Abraham Ortelius **published an atlas** called *The Theater of the World*. It showed countries that Europeans had not always known about, and was a huge best-seller!

1609 An Italian scientist called Galileo Galilei invented a new telescope. It helped him make **important discoveries** about how our planet moves around the sun.

Hooke observed that living things like leaves seemed to be made up of tiny "cells"

Curved mirror inside the tube brings light beams together

Eyepiece

Telescope turns on wooden ball

Telescope ▲

In 1668, sixty years after the first telescope was invented, English scientist Sir Isaac Newton created a new kind of telescope. It was called a reflector and used a mirror to collect light. It made things appear 40 times bigger—perfect for looking at distant planets and stars.

Eyepiece

◄ Small discoveries

Multi-talented scientist Robert Hooke built one of the first-ever microscopes. It was designed to zoom in on living things to see what they were made of. It made tiny insects and seeds look huge!

Screw turns to focus on the specimen

Build it!

LEGO Technic pin

Tilt technique

LEGO® Technic pins link the body of the microscope—built using a round brick with holes—with stands on either side, allowing it to tilt.

Bar with clip and stud

2x2 round jumper plate

Tick tock
Each hand of the clock is a bar with clip and stud. The hands can be moved to show different minutes and hours.

Build it!

Clock face shows time

Pendulum swings back and forth

Telling time ▶
The first clock that could tell time to within a few seconds was invented in 1657 by a Dutch scientist called Christiaan Huygens. It used a heavy weight called a pendulum, which swung from side to side in a very regular rhythm.

The sun casts a shadow on the horizon vane

Sight vane shows the sailor their position

Sailor lines the horizon vane up with the real horizon

◀ Navigation tool
In 1594, more and more explorers were setting sail to find distant new lands. An English sailor called John Davis invented the backstaff, a device that used the shadow cast by the sun to help ships keep to their routes.

Myths and legends

Discovering gravity
Scientific genius Sir Isaac Newton was also the first person to describe gravity, the invisible force that pulls things to the ground. According to legend, this brilliant idea came to him after an apple fell from a tree and hit him on the head!

I'VE GOT A BRAINWAVE ... AND A HEADACHE.

The force of gravity pulls the apple down to earth

Time of creativity

All over Europe, and especially in Italian cities like Florence and Rome, artists were busy making new, exciting creations. Writers, sculptors, musicians, and painters were inspired by changes in other areas of life, such as politics and science.

Brick bird

A brick with studs on all sides forms the body of each stone bird. This allows for two wings, a tail, and a head to be added.

Flame piece for wing

Brick with side scroll for head

Build it!

Figures were often much larger than life size

Cool fountains were popular in warm cities like Rome

Key moments

1503 Leonardo da Vinci began one of his most famous paintings, the *Mona Lisa*. It took him **14 years to finish** his masterpiece—either he was a perfectionist, or very, very busy!

1504 A statue of the biblical king David, by Michelangelo, went on display in the city of Florence. Today, over a million people a year **visit the museum** where David is kept.

Statues and sculpture ▲

Sculptors created grand statues and fountains for city squares and public places. Many were made from marble and showed gods, goddesses, and creatures from ancient mythology.

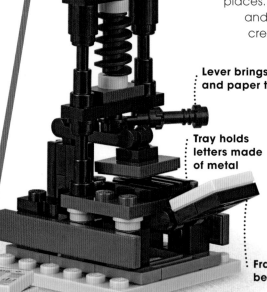

Lever brings type and paper together

Tray holds letters made of metal

◄ Books for all

When the first mechanical printing presses were developed, it meant books could be produced much more quickly and cheaply—making it easier for writers and thinkers to spread their new ideas.

Frame holds paper before and after printing

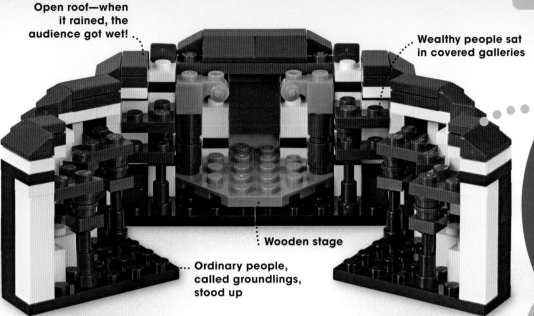

Open roof—when it rained, the audience got wet!

Wealthy people sat in covered galleries

Wooden stage

Ordinary people, called groundlings, stood up

Opening right
Hinge plates are hidden under the roof on either side of the stage. This allows the model to open up and reveal the inside of the theater.

Hinge plates

Build it!

▲ On stage

London's Globe Theatre put on the plays of William Shakespeare. Going to the theater was a popular pastime. More than 2,000 people would cram in to see the latest play—cheering, booing, chatting, eating, and drinking!

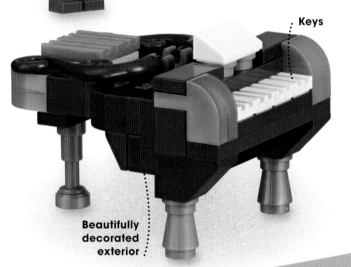

Keys

Beautifully decorated exterior

ALL THE WORLD'S A STAGE, ESPECIALLY AT THE GLOBE!

◄ Making music

The harpsichord was the most fashionable musical instrument in Europe at this time. It was a cross between a piano and a guitar—when you pressed the keys, it plucked its own strings, making a sharp, clear sound.

Elsewhere in the world

Music in Japan

In Japanese theater, actors wore dramatic, masklike makeup. The music was played on the shamisen, a kind of guitar with a very long neck.

Three strings make a chiming sound

Pegs turned to tune the strings

Age of industry

This was an age when people got busy—very busy! Machines were invented that could do things much faster than people could. Cities were filled with factories that completely changed the way people worked. No wonder it's called the Industrial Revolution!

Wheel turns the spindles

1764
Spinning jenny
In the UK, James Hargreaves invented a machine that spun cotton thread much faster than a human worker. He called it a jenny, short for engine. This was the start of the Industrial Revolution!

1810
Fight for Mexican independence
After years of Spanish rule, the Mexican people started a rebellion and gained their independence in 1821. This inspired other countries to do the same.

Modern stethoscopes have two earplugs and a chest piece

1816
Stethoscope
French doctor René Laennec developed a simple wooden tube to help him hear his patients' heartbeats.

1823
Early computer
In England, Charles Babbage designed an automatic mechanical calculator he called the Difference Engine. Although he never built it, we now know that his early computer design would have worked perfectly!

1848
Gold rush
After a farmer found gold in California, more than 300,000 people grabbed their shovels and headed for the hills. They all hoped to dig up a fortune for themselves!

I SURE HOPE IT IS A GOLDEN AGE FOR ME!

1885
Benz car
German engineer Karl Benz invented the first gasoline-powered car. It only had three wheels and didn't go very fast!

1891
Trans-Siberian railroad
In Russia, work began on a railroad linking Moscow to Vladivostok, 5,700 miles (10,000 km) away. It's still the world's longest railroad line.

Detectives used magnifying glasses to look for fingerprints ...

1892
Crime-fighting breakthrough
Argentinian police were the first to solve a crime using fingerprint science. They tracked down a criminal from a print left on a door.

Steam-powered locomotive

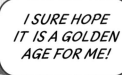

The Declaration of Independence was written in a house in Philadelphia

Let the light in
Use headlight bricks to create microscale windows. Make sure the side studs point inward to give the look of square windows.

1x1 headlight brick ....

Abraham Lincoln, President of the United States, 1861–1865 ....

Build it!

WHAT A MONUMENTAL TIME PERIOD.

1776
US independence
On the 4th of July, the Declaration of Independence was made and the US started forming its own government.

1783
Hot-air balloon
The first hot-air balloon was launched with no passengers. At the second launch in Paris, it had a crew of a duck, a chicken, and a sheep. The inventors were too nervous to test the balloon themselves!

.... Prisoners were in leg irons during the voyage

1788
Australian settlers
About 1,500 British prisoners and their guards arrive in Australia after sailing from England. Together, they set up a new British outpost.

1789
Start of the French Revolution
In Paris, people protested about how they were treated. They decided to seize power from the king and rule France for themselves.

The French revolutionary badge is called a cockade

1851
Great Exhibition
In London, England, crowds came to a giant glass building called the Crystal Palace to see the Great Exhibition. It was full of wonders from all over the world.

1859
Louis Pasteur
French scientist Louis Pasteur discovered that some diseases are caused by tiny organisms called bacteria (germs). His findings helped prevent diseases and save lives.

1873
Blue jeans
The first denim pants were made for US workers who needed hard-wearing clothing.

1876
First telephone
The inventor Alexander Graham Bell made the first ever telephone call—to his assistant in the next room!

1883
Krakatoa eruption
When the volcano on the island of Java (now in Indonesia) erupted, the gigantic explosion was heard 3,000 miles (4,800 km) away.

Hot liquid rock is called lava

.... The palace was made up of 300,000 panes of glass

1x2 plate with bars

Go with the flow
Attach plates with clips to plates with bars to create a sloped path for the lava. Pile transparent red, orange, and yellow elements on top of the plates.

.... 1x2 plate with clip

Build it!

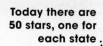

Today there are 50 stars, one for each state

The American Revolution

Stars and stripes ▲

The American flag was created in 1777. It had 13 stripes, to stand for the original settlements (called colonies) and 13 stars, one for each of the states in the newly formed US.

In 1765, America was still a part of Britain, but the people who lived there wanted to rule themselves. Eight years later, after many battles, the two sides agreed to make peace and a brand-new country was born— the United States of America!

Ships called tea clippers transported tea across the ocean

Boston Tea Party ▶

People in America were angry about having to pay taxes to Britain. In 1773, rebels boarded British ships in Boston Harbor and threw their cargo of tea overboard in protest!

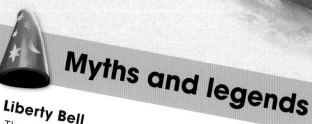

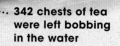

Myths and legends

342 chests of tea were left bobbing in the water

Liberty Bell

The Liberty Bell is one of the most famous symbols of the Revolution. According to legend, it was rung on July 4, 1776, to celebrate American independence. Nobody knows whether this really happened!

The bell hangs from a wooden beam

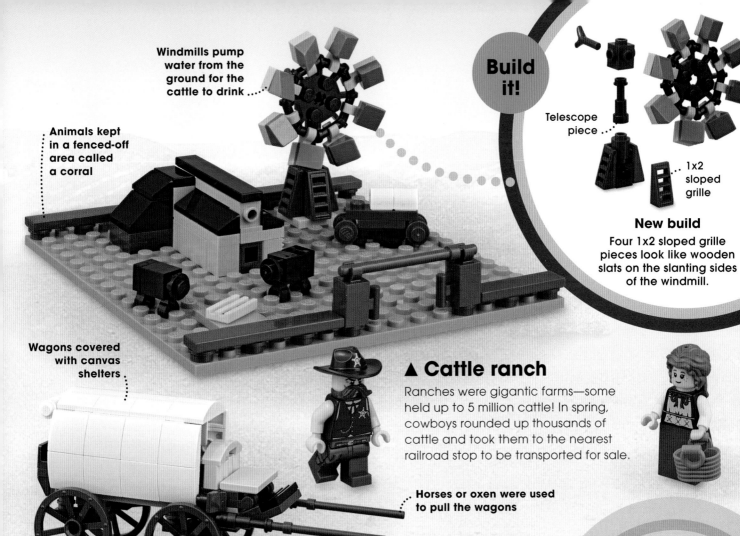

Windmills pump water from the ground for the cattle to drink ....

Animals kept in a fenced-off area called a corral

Build it!

Telescope piece ....

1x2 sloped grille

New build
Four 1x2 sloped grille pieces look like wooden slats on the slanting sides of the windmill.

Wagons covered with canvas shelters .

▲ Cattle ranch
Ranches were gigantic farms—some held up to 5 million cattle! In spring, cowboys rounded up thousands of cattle and took them to the nearest railroad stop to be transported for sale.

Horses or oxen were used to pull the wagons

▲ Wagon trail
Families from the east coast of America crammed everything they owned into wagons and set off for a new life in the west. Hundreds of wagons would travel together on the long, hard, and dangerous journey.

Where in the world?

The Wild West

Key moment

1862 To encourage people to move west, the government proclaimed that pioneers could have **land for free**, as long as they built a home and farmed their land for at least five years.

The US was a huge country. Thousands of people from the crowded east coast headed to the vast, empty lands in the west. They wanted to find their fortunes as farmers, cattle ranchers, or gold miners.

45

Gas lamp ▼

In towns and cities, the streets were lit by gas lamps. Every evening, a lamplighter had to light each lamp. In the morning, he came around to put them out again!

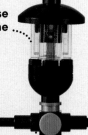

Glass case protects flame ·····

Rest for the lamplighter's ladder ·····

The Industrial Revolution

The age of machines and factories began in Britain, but soon spread to other countries. People moved from the countryside to cities, making them bigger, busier, and noisier as steam whooshed, machines clattered, engines clanged, and furnaces roared!

Key moments

1825 As more and more people moved to London to work in factories, it overtook Beijing as the **world's biggest city**, with 1.35 million people living there.

1833 In Britain, a new law **banned younger children** from factory work. From now on, workers had to be at least nine years old!

Steam pushes the metal beam up and down ·····

Beam makes the flywheel spin

▲ Steam engine

Scottish inventor James Watt made a steam engine that heated water and pumped jets of steam to make the parts move. Soon, his clever invention was driving machines in mines, mills, and factories.

THE WORLD IS REALLY STEAMING ALONG NOW!

1x1 corner wall panel

1x1 headlight brick

Clear windows
Make a row of square factory windows using headlight bricks facing into the building. Thin wall panels form the other factory walls.

Build it!

Train carries goods to and from the city

Factory life ▶

Huge buildings called factories were built to make things such as cloth using the newly invented machines. Hundreds of people worked day and night making goods in these early factories.

Water wheel to power machines

Car to carry passengers or freight

ALL ABOARD THE TEN PAST NINE TRAIN TO LONDON.

▶ Steam train

In the 1840s, people went crazy for building railroads—in the UK, they called the trend Railway Mania! Powerful trains were soon puffing around everywhere, from Australia to the US.

Elsewhere in the world

Hot-air balloon
After the Montgolfier brothers invented a hot-air balloon in 1783, people could travel by air for the first time. On the first flight with pilots, the balloon traveled about 6 miles (9 km) over Paris before coming down with a bump!

Gas fire to heat the air in the balloon

Time of construction

In the 1800s, business was booming! Space was getting tight as more people moved to crowded cities for work. People needed better, faster ways to travel and communicate. It was time for clever constructors and awesome engineers to get to work and build a modern, exciting world!

Key moments

1884 The **first steel-framed skyscraper** was the Home Insurance Building in Chicago. It was 138 ft (42 m) high and had 10 stories.

1866 Engineers on the SS Great Eastern laid a 2,000-mile-(3,200-km-) long **telegraph cable** along the bottom of the Atlantic Ocean.

Skyscrapers ▼

Tall, thin buildings began to be built in big cities. They were made with steel frames, rather than heavy bricks. This meant that they could be built taller than ordinary buildings and more people could live or work within them.

Workers perched on the girders to screw them together—often without harnesses!

Girders sunk deep into the ground for stability

Bar holder with clip

Building aid
A small section of 1x1 bricks is carried by a frame of bars and bar holders with clips.

Build it!

WHAT'S THE WEATHER LIKE UP THERE?

Suspension bridge ▶

Engineers used iron and steel to construct new bridges that could carry heavy loads over wide stretches of water. A bridge in which the deck is hung from strong cables is called a suspension bridge.

Tall tower at each end

Roadway (called the deck) hangs from strong metal chains

Six masts and five funnels

692 ft (211 m) long

▲ Brunel's boat

British engineer Isambard Kingdom Brunel built mighty steam ships, such as the SS *Great Eastern*, to carry goods and passengers between Britain and the US.

Build it!

1x2 brick with hole

LEGO ship's wheel

Watertight construction

The only hole in the ship's solid hull is the perfect fit for the pin on the back of a LEGO® ship's wheel.

◀ Sending news

In the 1830s, people started using cables to send messages over long distances. The sender tapped out signals in a code of clicks, which were picked up and decoded at the other end.

Wooden poles held the copper telegraph cables

Cables often ran alongside railroad tracks

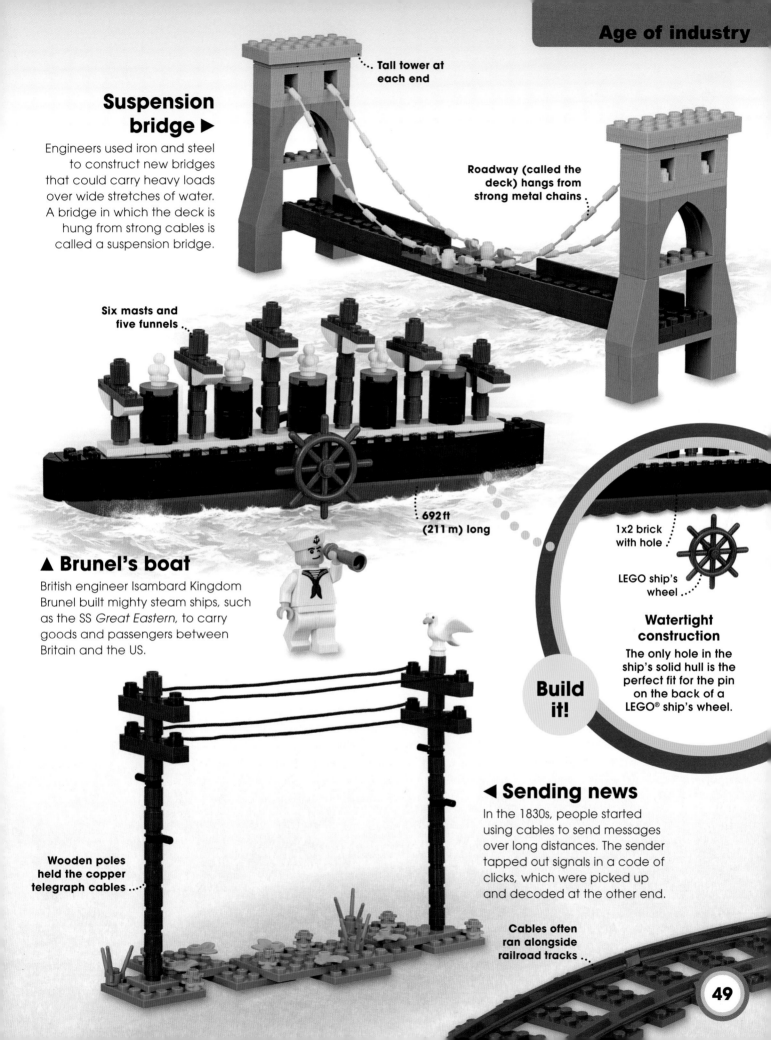

Exciting inventions

The late 1800s was a period when inventors and scientists made some amazing new creations. Their ingenious ideas meant that life in the next century would be very different—with bright lights, faster transportation, and new gadgets that meant less hard work for ordinary people.

Key moments

1873 Typewriters could print letters onto paper much **faster than humans could write**. The layout of the keys on the first typewriter was the same as on the computer keyboards we use today.

1901 Before vacuum cleaners, it was hard work to keep floors and carpets clean with just a broom. The **earliest vacuum cleaner machine** was so huge that it was pulled between houses by a horse!

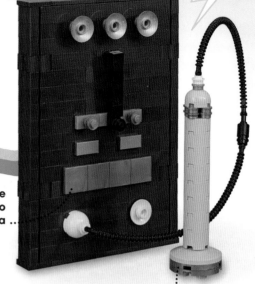

RING! RING!

Brass plate dedicated to Queen Victoria …

Telephone ▲

The telephone was an instant success when it was introduced in 1876. When the inventor, Alexander Graham Bell, showed this model to Queen Victoria, she was so impressed that she wanted to buy one!

Callers spoke into the receiver, then held it to their ear to hear the reply

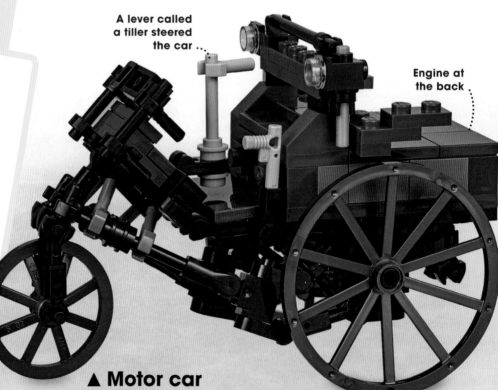

A lever called a tiller steered the car …

Engine at the back

▲ Motor car

The first motor car, developed in Germany by Karl Benz in 1885, had three wheels and a top speed of 10 mph (16 kph). By 1895, Benz had made and sold 130 models. Today there are more than a billion cars on the road.

The first car had bicycle wheels

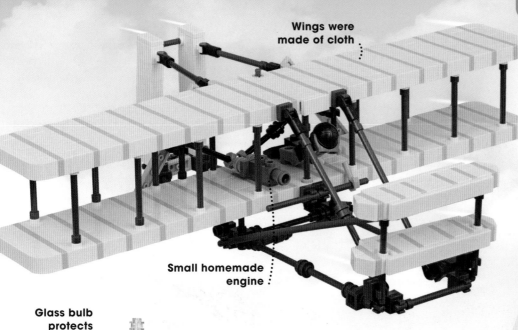

Wings were made of cloth

Small homemade engine

◀ First flight

In 1903, American brothers Orville and Wilbur Wright built the first-ever airplane, called *Wright Flyer* I. There was no cockpit—the pilot had to lie flat on the lower wing to steer the plane.

1x1 slope

Build it!

Sitting easy

The motor sits in the frame but does not connect to it. Build a shallow dip using small sloped pieces.

Glass bulb protects filament

◀ Bright idea

When the light bulb was invented, it lit up homes all over the world. Electric light was brighter, cleaner, and safer than candles and gas or oil lamps.

Wires deliver electricity to heat the filament

Brass frame

Machines could be attached to the turning rotor

▲ Electric motor

Serbian-American inventor Nikola Tesla discovered that machines worked better when the flow of electricity went back and forth. He used this to invent a new kind of electric motor, which still keeps our world running today!

Transparent globe

Clear creation

Clear transparent pieces are key to creating this LEGO light bulb with a visible filament. If you don't have clear pieces, try using white or yellow ones instead.

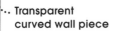

Transparent curved wall piece

Build it!

The modern world

Today, the world moves so fast that it's hard to keep up! Technology has changed how we communicate and new medicines mean we are healthier than ever. Most importantly, we have begun to understand how fragile our precious planet is and that we all need to take much better care of it.

1901
Australian independence
Australia became a federation, with its own national flag, Prime Minister, and parliament.

1903
Wright Brothers
In the US, Wilbur and Orville Wright made the first flight in an airplane. The flight only lasted a few seconds, but it was a start!

1928
Medical marvel
Penicillin was discovered by Scottish scientist Alexander Fleming. This medicine has saved the lives of millions of people by curing infections.

.. **Penicillin can be injected or taken as tablets**

1946
First computer
ENIAC, the first electronic computer, was developed in the US. It filled a whole room and weighed the same as five elephants!

1955
Hovercraft
The hovercraft was designed to skim over water, land, or ice on a huge, inflatable cushion of air.

.. **Cushion is called a skirt**

1958
NASA founded
The National Aeronautics and Space Administration (NASA) was founded in the United States. It was a reaction to a successful rocket launch in Russia the year before.

Launch tower ...

2011
Population boom
In October 2011, the world's population reached 7 billion people. One hundred years earlier, there were only 1.7 billion people on the whole planet.

2014
Comet landing
The European space probe, Rosetta, landed a craft called Philae on a speeding comet. The craft is investigating what comets are made of.

.. **Philae is the size of a washing machine**

2019
Climate change
Young people around the world took part in school strikes to protest against climate change. The movement was led by 16-year-old activist Greta Thunberg from Sweden.

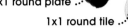

Dial rotated to enter numbers

1907
Fantastic plastic
Bakelite was the first plastic to be created. It was used to make furniture, music records, and jewelry.

Wooden wheels

1908
Car crazy
In the US, the model T Ford was the first car that ordinary people could afford to buy. The road revolution had begun!

1912
Titanic
Designed to be the biggest, safest cruise ship ever, the *Titanic* sank on its very first voyage after hitting a huge iceberg.

There were 10 decks and 840 cabins on the *Titanic*

1925
Television invented
Scottish inventor John Logie Baird's first TV only showed black and white pictures. He developed color television three years later.

1961
First human in space
Russian pilot Yuri Gagarin was the first person to see Earth from space, in his rocket Vostok 1. When he landed, Yuri was a hero!

Antenna sends and receives signals

1973
First cell phone
The earliest cell phones were big and heavy and the battery only lasted for an hour.

1990
First website
The World Wide Web was developed by English computer scientist Sir Tim Berners-Lee. It was an easy-to-use system that made the internet available to everyone.

2000
International Space Station
Scientists live and carry out experiments on the Space Station. The ISS orbits the Earth 16 times every day.

1969
Man on the moon
US astronaut Neil Armstrong, commander of the Apollo 11 mission, became the first human to walk on the moon.

I'M TAKING ONE GIANT LEAP FOR BRICK-KIND!

We can now browse over one billion websites on the internet

Solar panels power the ISS

Radio time ▼

In the 1920s, radio was an exciting new form of entertainment. Around the world, whole families would gather around the large radio set to listen to live news, comedy, and music shows.

Dial to change between programs

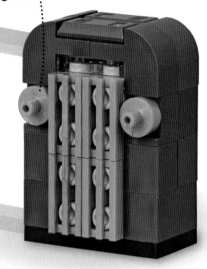

Cinema and entertainment

The 1900s were a time for entertaining! Listening to the radio at home or going to the cinema to see the latest films were favorite activities. The center of the new movie industry was Hollywood, where the dry, sunny weather made it perfect for filming all year.

Reels of film

Glass lens focuses the image ....

Sturdy legs keep camera steady

◄ Moving pictures

Early movie cameras worked by taking many photos (frames) every second and storing them on long strips of film. When the film was played back, the frames moved so quickly that the pictures looked as if they were moving.

Tiny screen showed moving images .....

Key moment

1939 The film *Gone with the Wind* had its premiere. It is still the **biggest money-making movie of all time**. Allowing for rising prices, it has earned the equivalent of 3.7 billion dollars!

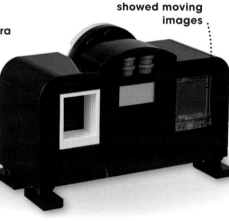

Build it!

4x4 round brick

.... **2x2 curved tile**

LEGO Technic friction pin

Make a film

Tiles attach to a round brick to create a film reel. Attach the reels to the camera with LEGO® Technic friction pins.

▲ First televisions

TVs first went on sale in the late 1920s. The first machines were called televisors. There was only one channel, the picture was fuzzy, and you couldn't watch pictures and hear sound at the same time. But it was a start!

Large speakers boom out over the parking area

▲ Drive-in movies

In the US, drive-in movie theaters were open-air cinemas where you watched films from the comfort of your own car. People could buy popcorn and hotdogs—but they had to watch out for bugs, attracted by the lights!

Elsewhere in the world

Business in Bollywood

During the golden age of Hollywood, the Indian movie business—or "Bollywood"—was also booming. Based in Mumbai, the industry began in the age of silent movies, and became famous for historical epics and lavish musicals. Today, Bollywood is the largest film-making center in the world.

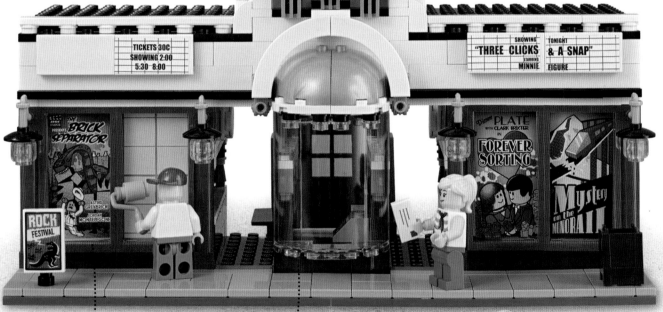

TICKETS 30C
SHOWING 2:00
5:30 8:00

SHOWING "THREE CLICKS" STARRING MINNIE

TONIGHT & A SNAP FIGURE

Posters advertised coming movies

Ticket booth

▲ At the movies

Cinemas were so fancy that they were called "picture palaces." Neon lights and lavish decorations created a magical atmosphere for people to escape from the real world into a fantasy land.

AND THE BEST PICTURE IS ...

... ANYTHING WITH ME IN IT!

I THOUGHT A SPACE WALK SOUNDED RELAXING!

Sputnik 1 ▶

In 1957, a small, silver satellite was the first human-made object to orbit the Earth. Sputnik 1 transmitted radio signals to let scientists on Earth know where it was.

Four antennas sent signals back to Earth

Body contained scientific sensors

The Space Race

In the 1950s, scientists built rockets that were powerful enough to reach space. From then, the race was on. Who would be the first country to send an astronaut into space? And who would win the biggest prize—and be the first human ever to walk on the moon?

Reentry capsule took Gagarin back to Earth

◀ Human space mission

In 1961, a Russian pilot called Yuri Gagarin became the first human in space when he orbited Earth in his craft, Vostok 1. After a 108-minute mission, he landed home safely and became a worldwide superstar!

Create a crater

Create a dip on a flat surface by building a raised ring of curved pieces. It will give the illusion of a crater!

... 2x2 quarter curved tile

... 2x2 quarter curved brick

▼ Man on the moon

In 1969, the US won the space race when pilot Neil Armstrong hopped off the ladder of his landing craft and made the first human footprint on the surface the moon! With his crewmate, Buzz Aldrin, he spent 22 hours exploring the moon.

The astronauts left a flag at the landing site

The moon's craters were made by falling meteorites

DID SOMEONE SAY FALLING METEORITES ...?

Build it!

Crew lived
in this
compartment

Solar panels
powered the
station

Space station ▶

In 1971, the Soviet Union launched Salyut 1, the first science lab in space. The crew orbited the Earth 383 times, carrying out different experiments.

Docking port
for rockets

Transparent
tile

1x2 plate
with clips

Space sections

Panels of different sizes attach to the model. They are made of plates with clips and bars, covered with transparent tiles.

Build it!

Antenna for TV
transmission

▼ Lunar rover

Later US moon missions took a vehicle along! The battery-powered buggy weighed just 475 lb (208 kg). In it, astronauts traveled up to 4.7 miles (7.6 km) from the lunar lander.

I HOPE I DON'T NEED A PARKING PERMIT.

Equipment
store

Key moments

1963 The **first woman in space** was Russian Valentina Tereshkova. Her trip lasted 3 days, and she's still the only woman ever to fly a solo space mission.

2007 Peggy Whitson became the first woman to command the International Space Station. She has spent a total of **665 days in space**—more than any other American astronaut.

Wire mesh
wheels

Technology jumps ahead

Over the past 50 years, scientists and engineers have made many brilliant breakthroughs. These new technological creations impact all parts of our lives, from keeping in contact to keeping the lights on!

Pin and spin

Give your drone spinning propellers by attaching LEGO propeller pieces using LEGO Technic pins. Raise them above the drone with round pieces.

- Propeller
- LEGO Technic pin
- 2x2 round tile with hole

Build it!

Speed of different rotors controls direction

Antenna sends and receives data

···· Mounted camera

▲ Flying drones

The first drones were built 100 years ago, but they looked more like balloons! Today, these mini flying robots can take photos, collect weather data, and even deliver pizzas! They can be controlled from the ground by remote control, or programmed before they take off.

Key moments

1982 The first **compact discs** (CDs) were developed. They could hold enough data to store music and videos, as well as computer files.

2011 The computer game *Minecraft* was developed in Sweden. It went on to become the **world's most played** computer game ever.

Antenna up to 7 in (18 cm) long ····

Earpiece and speaker

◀ Cell phones

Cell phones were first sold in shops in the 1980s. They were as big as bricks and weighed over 2 lb (1 kg)! Today's smartphones weigh much less than that, and can do everything a desktop computer can—and more.

···· Two keypads, for numbers and functions

Wind power ▶

In recent years, we have realized we need to use energy that doesn't run out or damage the planet. Renewable energy from wind, waves, and sunlight is gradually becoming our main source of power.

Generator converts movement into power

Rotor power

Create convincing turbine blades with a LEGO Technic rotor plate and white elements such as curved slopes.

LEGO Technic rotor plate

Rotors are turned by wind to make energy

1x4 curved slope

Wind turbines are often located in the sea, where it's windiest

Build it!

WOULD YOU LIKE A DRINK?

WHAT WILL WE INVENT NEXT, I WONDER?

Video cameras help robots navigate their surroundings

◀ Robot helpers

Robots are computers that can think and move for themselves. Cyber-technology has become more and more advanced over the last 20 years. Companion bots often look like humans and are programmed to help people with their daily tasks.

Monitor weighed more than 22 lb (10 kg)!

Home computers ▶

The first home computers were kits that you had to put together yourself! In the 1980s, the ready-made personal computer (PC) arrived—and so did computer games!

Files stored on portable floppy disks

Some robots can run, dance, and even play soccer!

Feet adjust to keep balance when walking

59

Modern cities

In ancient times, as described at the beginning of this book, there was no such thing as a village, let alone a city! Today, more people than ever live in cities, with millions more traveling in each day to work, study, or just to have fun and see the sights.

Apartment buildings for people to live in

Build it!

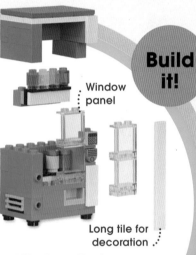

Window panel

Long tile for decoration

Window display

The vending machine is built as a box with shelves in the center. The front of the box is made of window pieces.

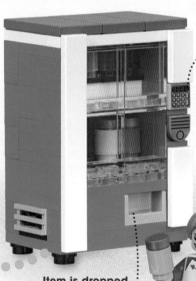

Item is dropped into the collection compartment

Customers pay with coins or by card

◀ Vending machines

The most common vending machines sell drinks and snacks, but in some cities you can find machines that sell books, clothes, freshly cooked fries, and even cars!

Transit systems ▼

Often the fastest way to get around a busy city is by going beneath it. London's 150-year-old underground system is the oldest in the world, and Beijing's is the busiest, carrying more than 10 million passengers every day.

In the rush hour, passengers cram into the cars

Slim trains fit through narrow tunnels

Key moments

2007 For the first time in the world's history, more than half of all people were **living in cities** rather than in the country.

2019 Tokyo became the **biggest city in history**, with a population of 37 million people.

Modern cities have buildings in different styles

◀ City skyline

When cities get bigger, they grow up as well as out. New technology makes it possible to build taller and taller structures for people to live and work in. The world's tallest office building—in Dubai—has 163 floors!

Ads designed to grab the attention of busy passersby

City lights ▶

Many cities have a place that's famous for bright lights and multicolored signs—New York City has Times Square, Shanghai has Nanjing Road, and Tokyo has Akihabara, which means "Electric Town."

Moving images on LED digital screens

I KNOW WHAT I WANT FOR DINNER ... PIZZA!

Build it!

Thin wall sits on jumper plate

Street slant

Build a wall at an angle by placing it on a single stud and surrounding it with smooth tiles.

1x2 jumper plate

1x1 stud

Meet the builders

The models in this book were created by a talented team of builders who love building with LEGO® bricks and pieces! We asked them to share some of their stories about building LEGO models.

Jason Briscoe

If you could time travel to a different historical period, when would it be?
Probably the Victorian era in Britain, because the engineering skill in everything they built is incredible. It was all done with paper, pencil, and old-fashioned mathematics, not a computer in sight ... Amazing.

What is your favorite build that you made for this book?
It has to be the movie theater. It evokes a bygone golden age of cinema, and I especially like the white and gold decoration on the front.

What is your favorite thing to build (other than history)?
Spaceships and futuristic space scenes.

How tidy is your brick collection? What's your top tip for keeping it tidy?
Ermmm, not very tidy ... I have semi-organized chaos ... My motto is that I'd rather be building than sorting and tidying bricks!

However, sorting by part type is the most sensible option if you have space and a large collection.

Movie theater

Nate Dias

If you could time travel to a different historical period, when would it be?

I would love to travel back to the Middle Ages. I love the idea of knights in shining armor, I love a castle, and it would be a dream come true to be one of Robin Hood's Merry Men.

What is your favorite build that you made for this book?

I think my favorite build has to be the Sphinx. I like how it turned out, looking like the actual Sphinx but with a playful cartoonlike expression.

What is your favorite thing to build (other than history)?

I like to build life-size objects and then hide them around places. I love to see people's reactions when they realize the item is actually a LEGO version.

Sphinx

How tidy is your brick collection? What's your top tip for keeping it tidy?

I have to admit that my brick collection could be tidier. Even though I sort my collection, it gets very messy when I start building (and I don't enjoy cleaning up afterward). I like to organize my collection by part. Collections sorted by color look prettier, but I find it more difficult to find the part I want. For example, if I want a red 1x3 brick, it's easier for me to see it in a box full of different 1x3 bricks than it would be for me to see it in a box full of red bricks.

Simon Pickard

Light bulb

If you could time travel to a different historical period, when would it be?

I would go back to the time of the Romans. I have always been keen on learning how people lived, especially the Romans. I even own a full set of Roman heavy infantry armor. It is just like the armor the Roman minifigures walking along my Roman road model are wearing!

What is your favorite build that you made for this book?

The light bulb was a particularly challenging shape to create in LEGO elements. It was the challenge of figuring out what was available and how this model could come together that I found enjoyable.

It was a bonus to discover that the parts I used meant the bulb is very close to its real size.

What is your favorite thing to build (other than history)?

Models based on the LEGO® Space subtheme, Blacktron.

How tidy is your brick collection? What's your top tip for keeping it tidy?

I have a highly organized storage system using toolbox sorting trays so that every part is separated into shape and color. The only way to keep it tidy is to make sure you put parts away every day.

Useful bricks

All LEGO® bricks are useful, but these are some that you might find particularly handy for a historical build. Don't worry if you don't have all of these parts. Get creative with the pieces you do have.

Brick basics

Bricks are the basis of most LEGO® builds. They come in many shapes and sizes, and are named according to size.

2x3 brick overhead view

2x3 brick side view

Plates are the same as bricks, only thinner. Three stacked plates are the same height as a standard brick.

1x2 plate

3 1x2 plates

1x2 brick

Tiles look like plates, but without any studs on top. This gives them a smooth look for more realistic builds.

2x2 tile   **2x2 round tile**

1x6 tile

Slopes are any bricks with diagonal angles. They can be big, small, curved, or inverted (upside down).

1x2 slope   **1x2 inverted slope**

1x3 curved slope

Cool connectors

Jumper plates allow you to "jump" the usual grid of LEGO studs. Use them to center things like flags or other decorations.

1x2 jumper plate

There are different kinds of **bricks with side studs**. They all allow you to build outward as well as upward.

1x1 brick with two side studs

1x2/2x2 angle plate

Plates with sockets and **plates with balls** link together to make flexible connections for things like vehicles and animals.

Ball joint socket   **2x2 brick with ball joint**

Any piece with a **bar** can fit onto a piece with a **clip**. Use clips and bars to make moving or angled features.

1x2 plate with bar

1x1 plate with clip

Hinge plates can give your builds side-to-side movement. **Hinge bricks** are used to tilt things up and down.

Hinge plates

1x2 hinge brick with 2x2 hinge plate

LEGO® Technic parts expand the range of functions you can build into your models.

LEGO Technic beam

LEGO Technic friction pin

For creatures

Printed 1x1 round tile for eye

1x1 slope for nose

Long bone piece for tusk

1x1 angled tooth plate

For buildings

2x2 dome

2x2 round textured brick

1x2 log brick

Arched, lattice window

1x4x2 arch

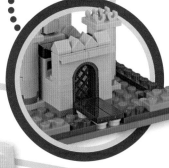

For vehicles

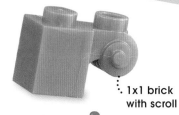

Cart wheel

Propeller

Ship's wheel

Angled plate for ship's sail

Train wheel

To decorate

1x1 brick with scroll

Flag

Flame

Gemstone

Plant

Ice cream piece for steam or smoke

Microfigure

Glossary

Hot-air balloon

Moai

Mayan temple

ancestor
A member of a family who lived a long time ago.

ancient
Very old. "Ancient history" describes the time from the first human settlements to when the Roman Empire ended.

armor
Strong covering that protects soldiers or vehicles in battle.

army
A large group of soldiers who are trained to fight in battles.

capital city
A country's most important city, usually where the government or ruler is based.

cargo
Goods carried from one place to another by a vehicle or by animals, such as horses or camels.

century
A period of 100 years. We live in the 21st century CE, which started in 2000 and will end in 2099.

civilization
The way of life of a group of people living in a particular area, for example the Inca civilization of South America.

communication
The ways people swap ideas or explain their thoughts. Writing and speaking are methods of communication.

conquer
To defeat a country or land and take control of it.

construction
Building new structures, for example palaces, or whole cities.

continent
A huge area of land. Earth has seven continents—Africa, Antarctica, Asia, Australia, Europe, North America, and South America.

discovery
Finding things that are new, for example a new land or a scientific breakthrough.

electricity
A type of power created by tiny particles called electrons. Electricity makes machines move. It can also produces light and heat.

empire
A group of lands or countries ruled by one government or person.

Steam train

Hunter's kayak

engineer
A person who uses science and math to build things or solve technical problems.

experiment
A test to see how something works. Scientists perform experiments to check if their ideas are correct.

explorer
Someone who goes on long journeys to discover new places and things.

government
A group of people who make the laws and run a country.

independence
When a country stops being controlled by another country and rules itself.

inventor
A person who creates a new idea or a product that changes the way we do things.

kingdom
A country or area ruled by a king or queen.

medieval
A period of history from around 500 CE to 1450 CE, which is also called the Middle Ages.

merchant
Someone whose job is to buy and sell goods.

monument
A building or structure put up to honor the memory of a famous person or important event.

rebellion
People joining together to fight against their own ruler or government.

settlement
A place a group of people move to and make their permanent home. A village is a small settlement; a city is a large settlement.

taxes
Money that people have to pay to their government to fund services like schools and hospitals.

technology
The use of knowledge to invent devices or tools that make life easier, or the tools themselves.

temple
A place where people gather to worship a god or goddess.

trade
Buying and selling goods, or exchanging them for other items.

tribe
A group of people who share the same history, language, and way of life.

warrior
A soldier, often one who is particularly highly skilled in combat.

Taj Mahal

Index

Fire

Space station

Viking longship

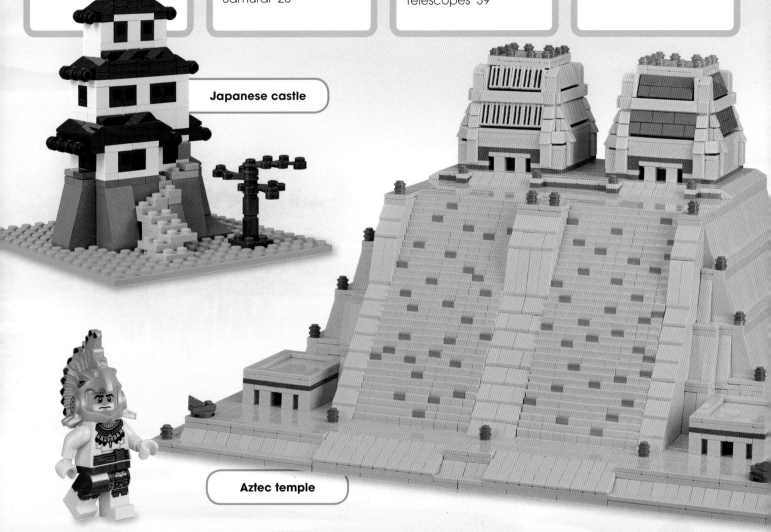

Japanese castle

Aztec temple